No Lines to Erase

By RL Lane

"There are no lines to erase," they said one night.

Then I thought of the picture on your cover.

I drew it back on December 2nd of 2014.

It is true I hardly ever erase when I am drawing.

Sometimes I draw something and then I draw over it.

The picture below is hidden forever…

It is an important message…

I told them I am not trying to erase anything. I just want to…

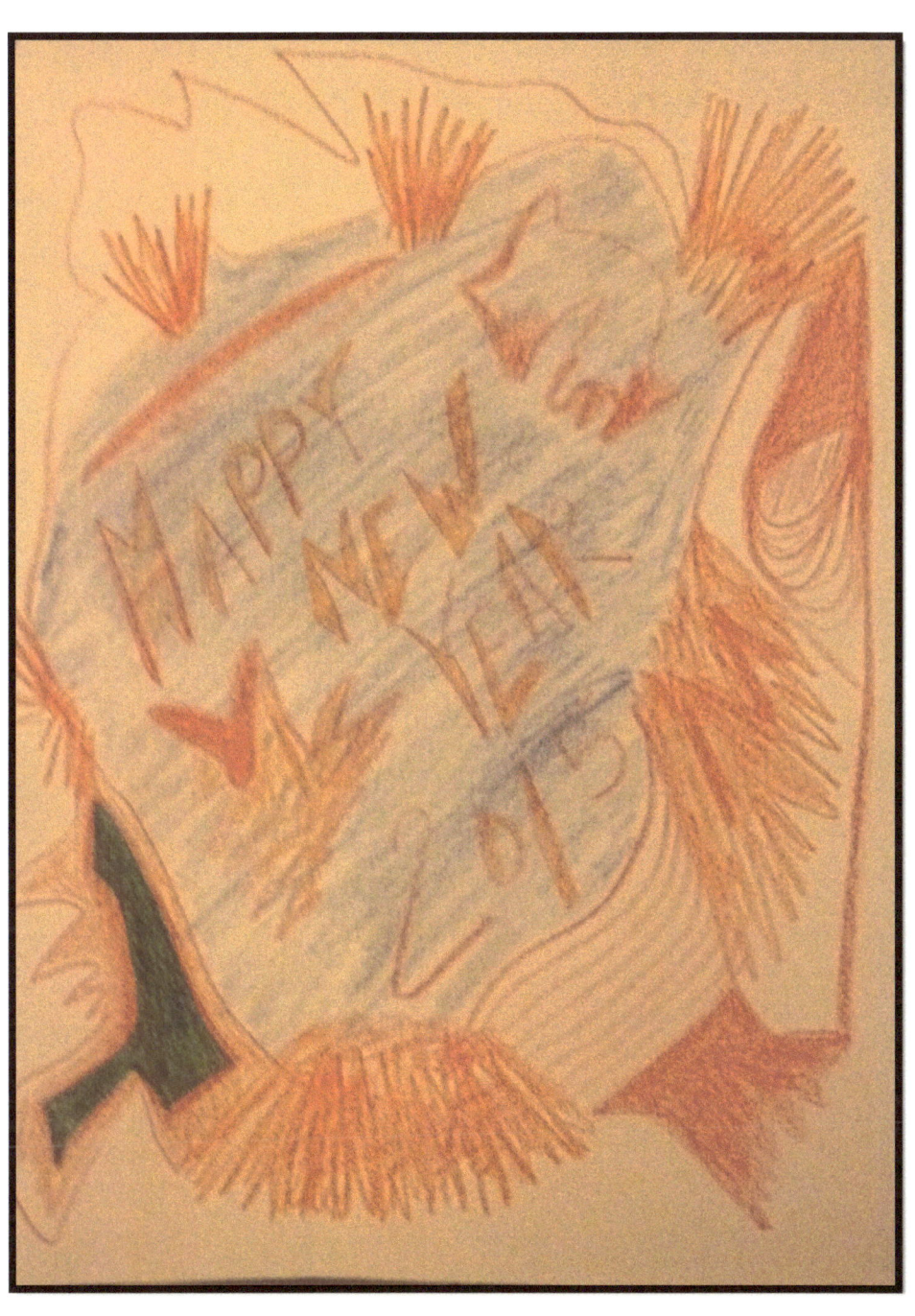

"You cannot change what you have done," they said. Flip the calendar and start anew…

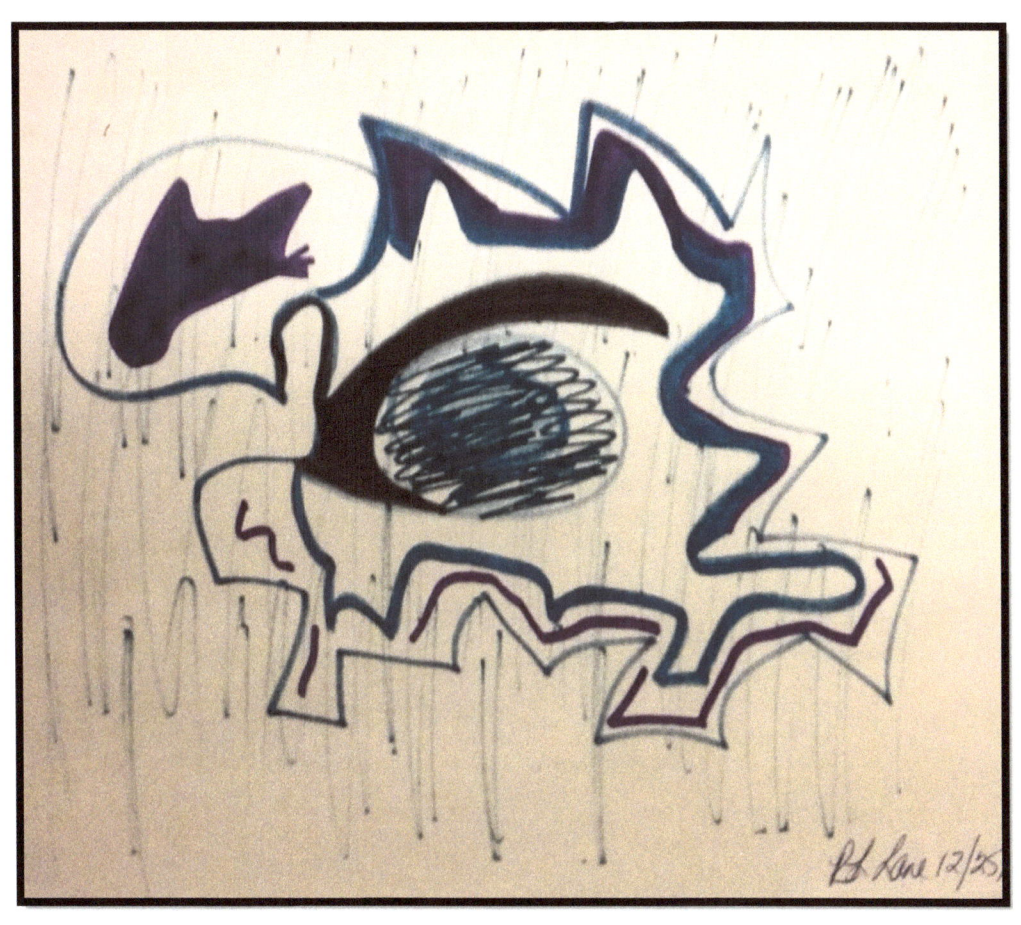

The game of cat and mouse. Is that what this picture is about? The eye that is always watching us… Watch your back…

In life, there are no lines to erase. You cannot change what you have done. You cannot just erase something like you can a line on a piece of paper.

Oh. Everyone knows that. They are trying to tell me something else…

The drawing on the cover. I was just following what they told me to do. I did not know what I was drawing. I see the parrot, the duck, the cow's head, and the fish. I remember struggling with the body of the duck. Where to connect the line. There is another animal below the cow's head. The whole picture is an owl looking through his monocle.

Oh. They are saying I can't erase. I could erase if I knew what I was drawing. I do not know what I am drawing. It is true. I just draw what they tell me…move my hand here and there and then around and then up and down until they tell me we are done…

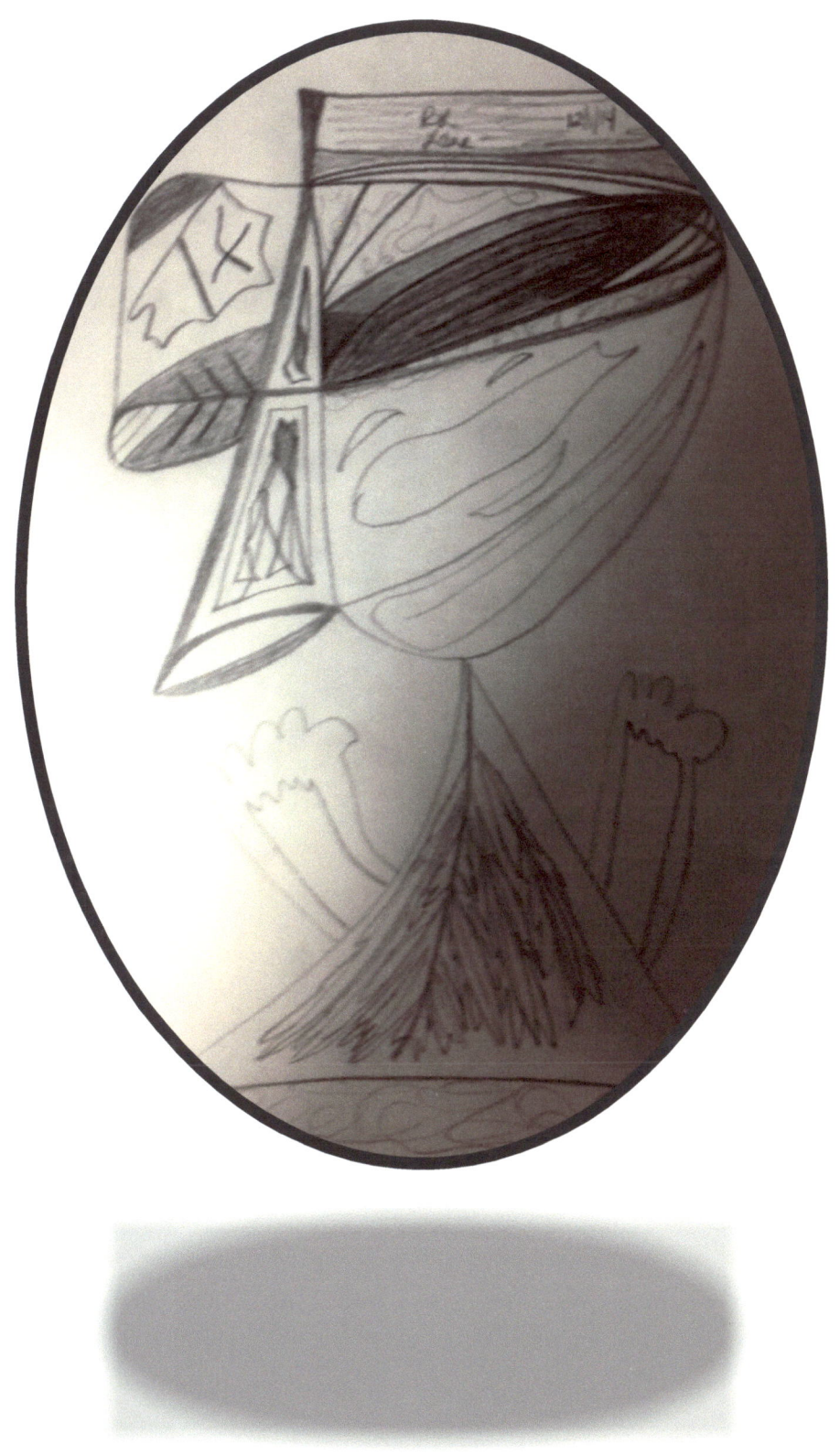

I drew "Santa" in December of 2014. Before the holiday. I didn't draw the light coming out of his headlamp. Somehow it just appeared when I took a picture of it...

I drew these with my eyes closed. On two separate days. I called them the "Moving Houses". I had realized at this point that I don't need to see what I am doing. I just feel the way to move...

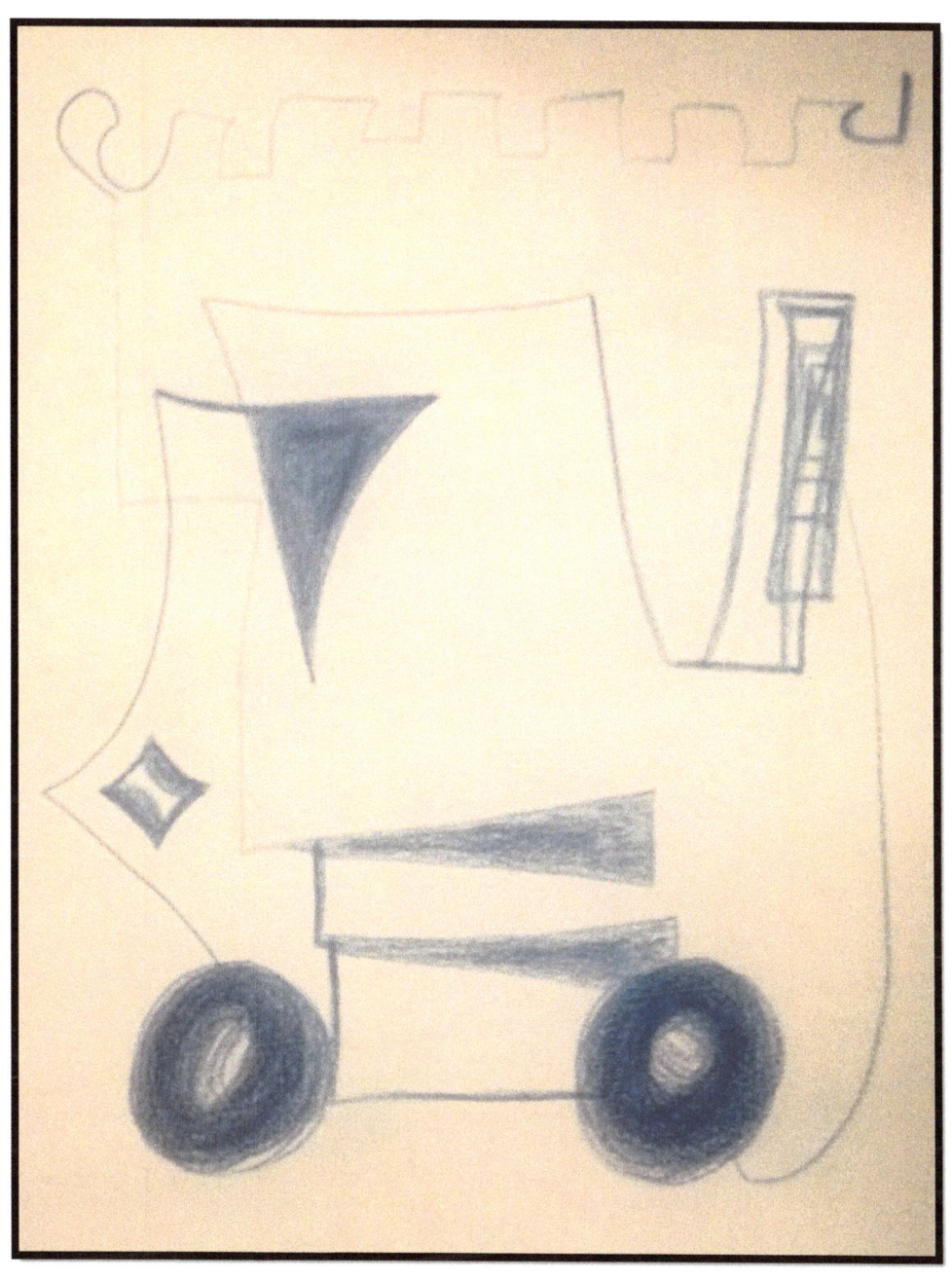

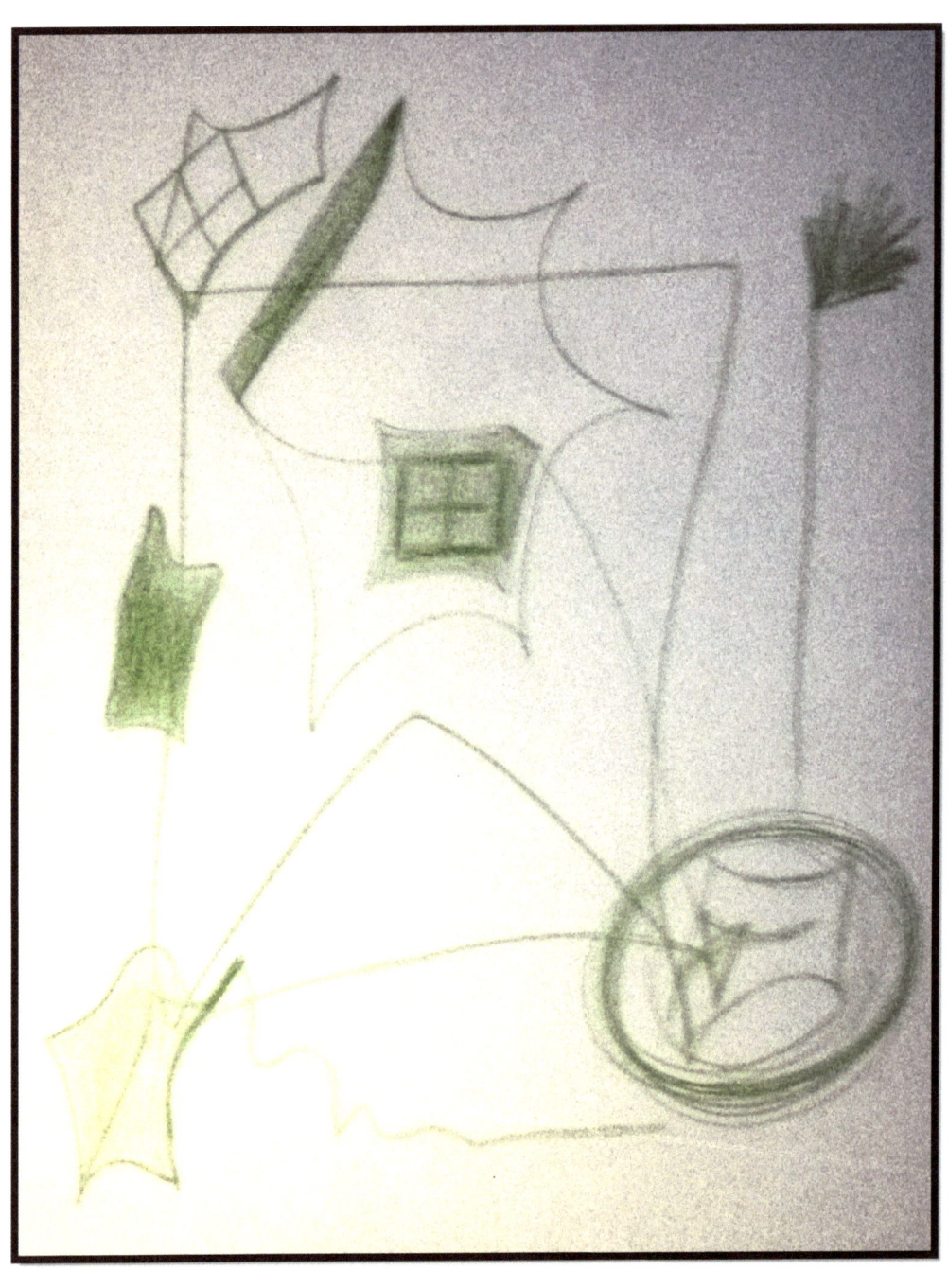

See the bright corner where the ghost is with his fishing pole…

Some people like the black and white sketches the best…

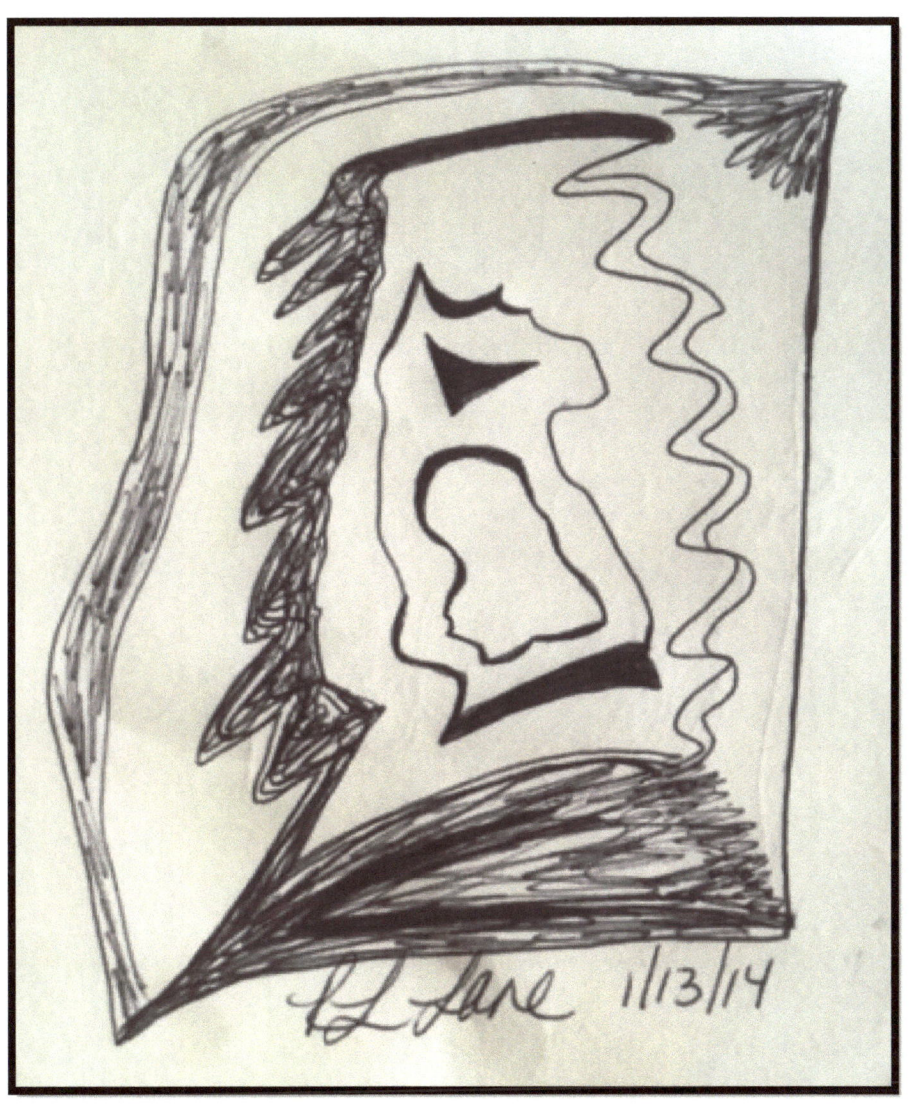

I called this the "Rocking Horse". You can see the smudge
marks from the ink on my hand. It makes me think of the Trojan Horse
and how the Greeks hid inside…waiting to attack. This one hasn't
made it into any of the books in the EcarreT series yet…

There are some pictures that are my personal favorites…

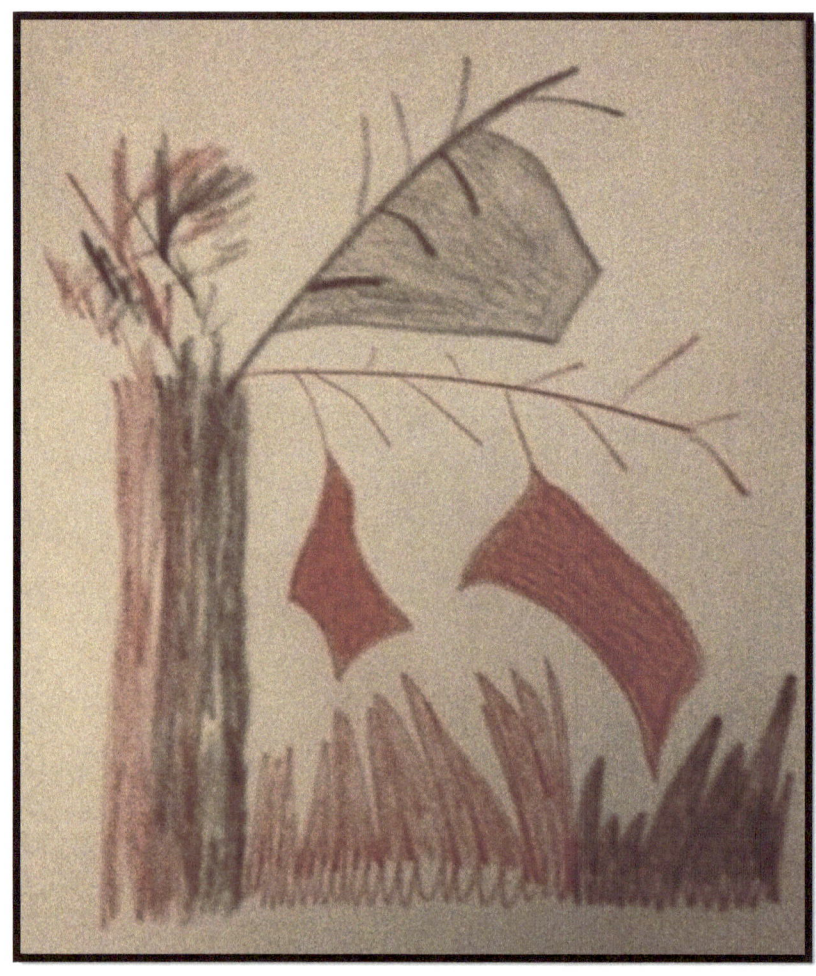

Red flags mean alert. I couldn't figure out why they were trying to alert me. Then finally I realized they are the red flags…like the ones used to wave the bullon…bull on. *Bouillon? My Dad did like his soups. I know this picture is tied to my Dad who loved our flag…*

I have drawn a lot of flags…

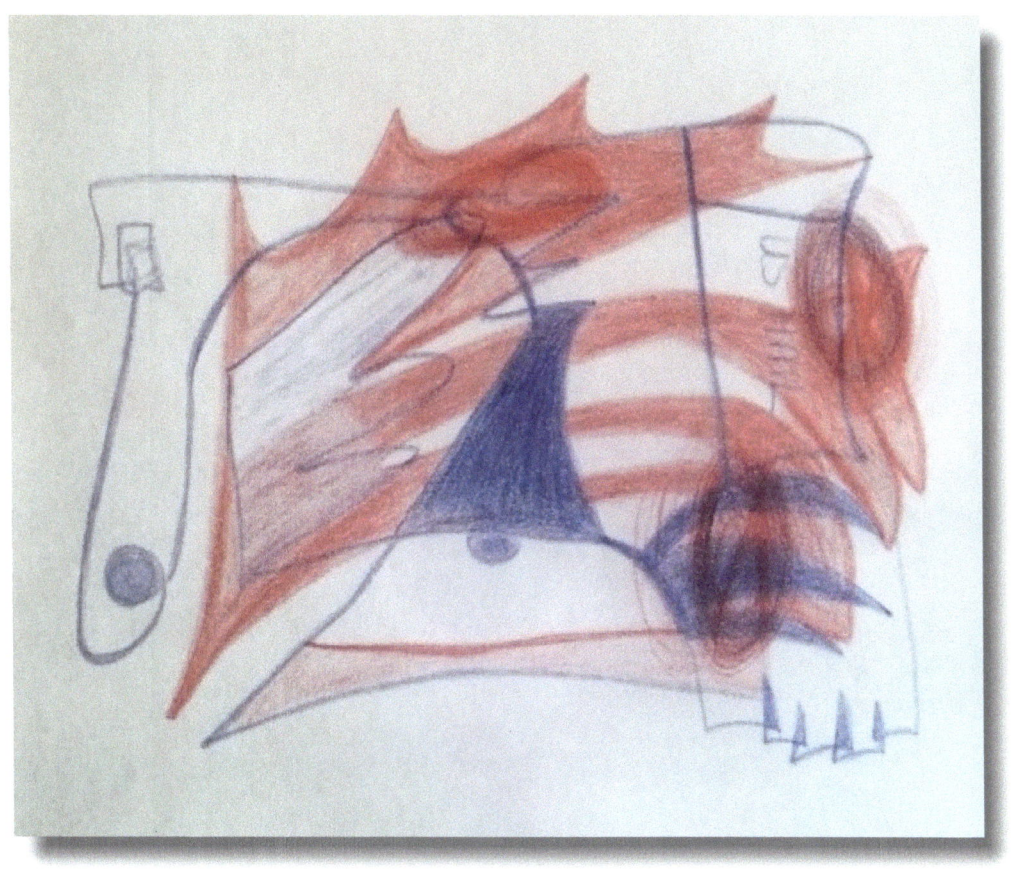

"The shredded flag"

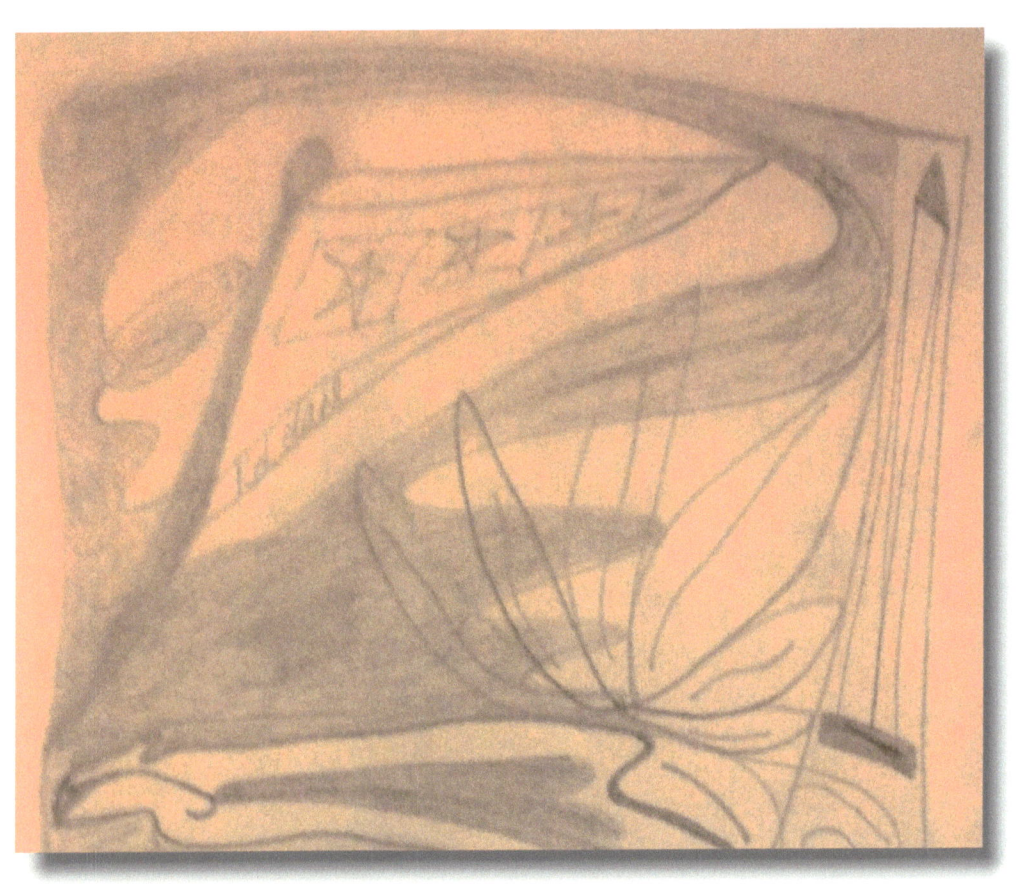

"The flag, the lily, the monument"

The Dad, the Mom, the Navy Doctor

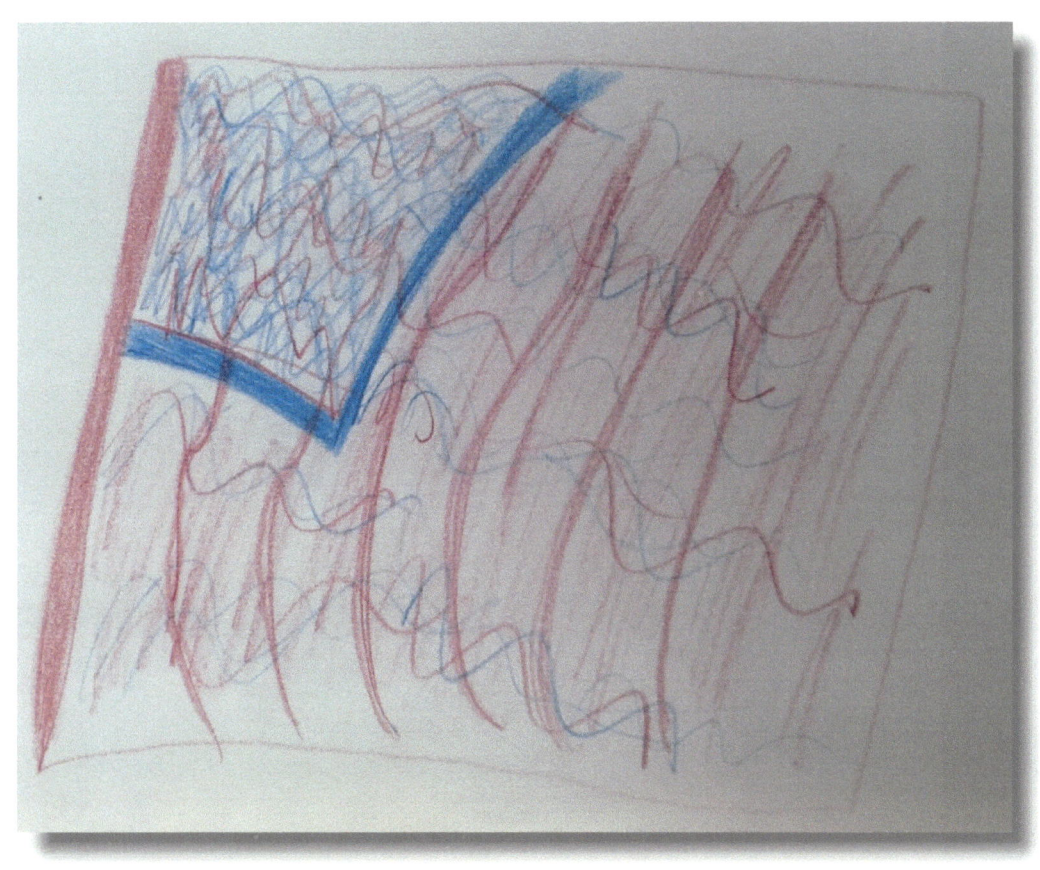

"The Waving Flag"

A lot of flags, a lot of flowers, a lot of birds…

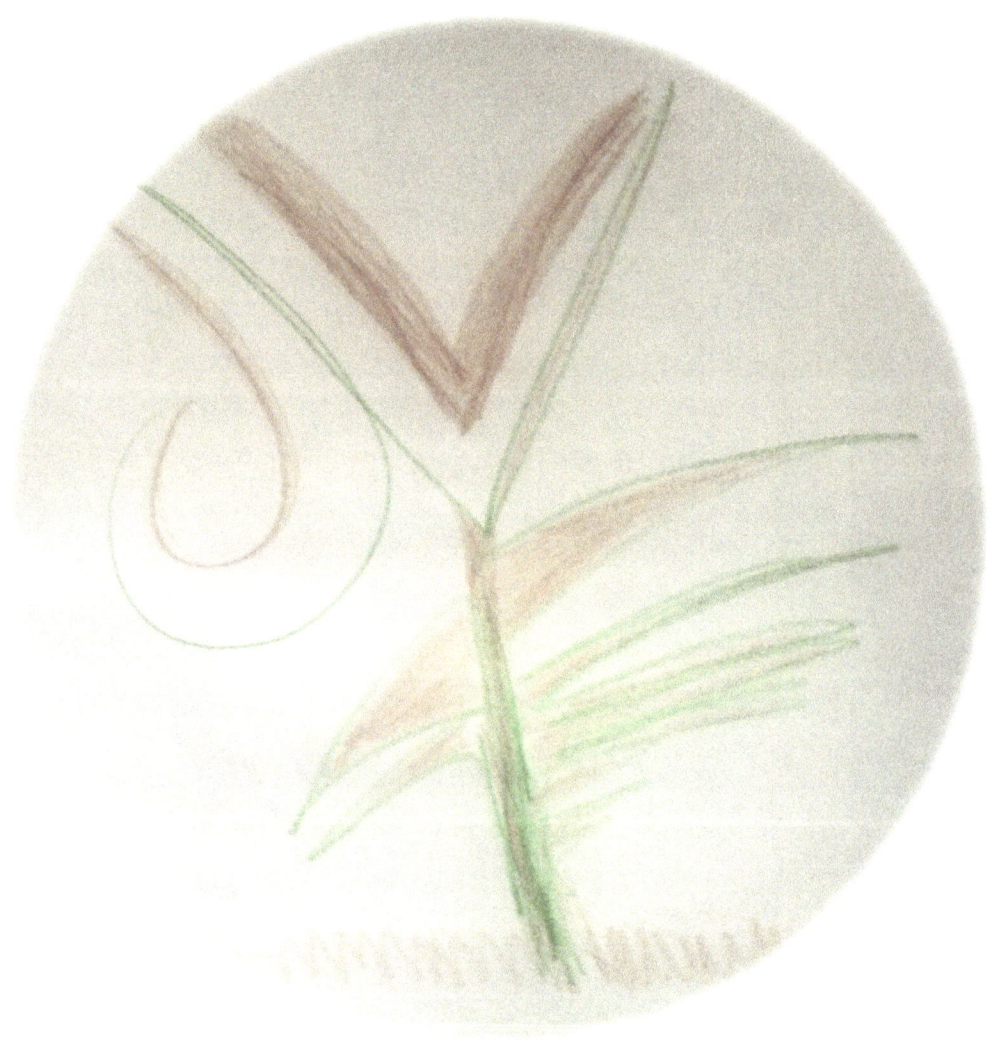

Is that the red-headed woodpecker down by the stem? He loved those too. The flower is his initials. J.V.

There is something different about this bird. It is actually really ugly, but something makes me like it. I feel like it is one of those drawings that I will look at one day and see the real picture…

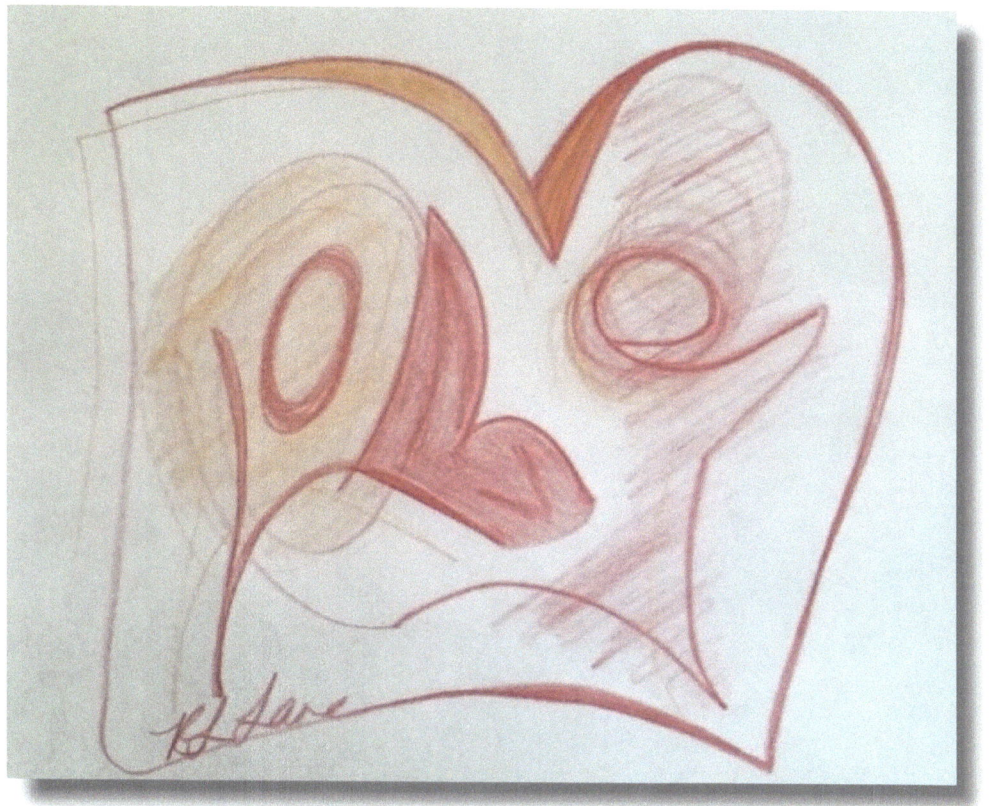

Oh. Is that the message to this one? Keep on looking at the ugly until you see the beautiful. Is there beautiful in every ugly? How long do you have to keep on trying to see it?

For me…that message is for me…

But the real message…for you… It is a good one to remember which is why I am writing it down. It'll probably help us at the end of our lives when we are hoping to go up and not down…

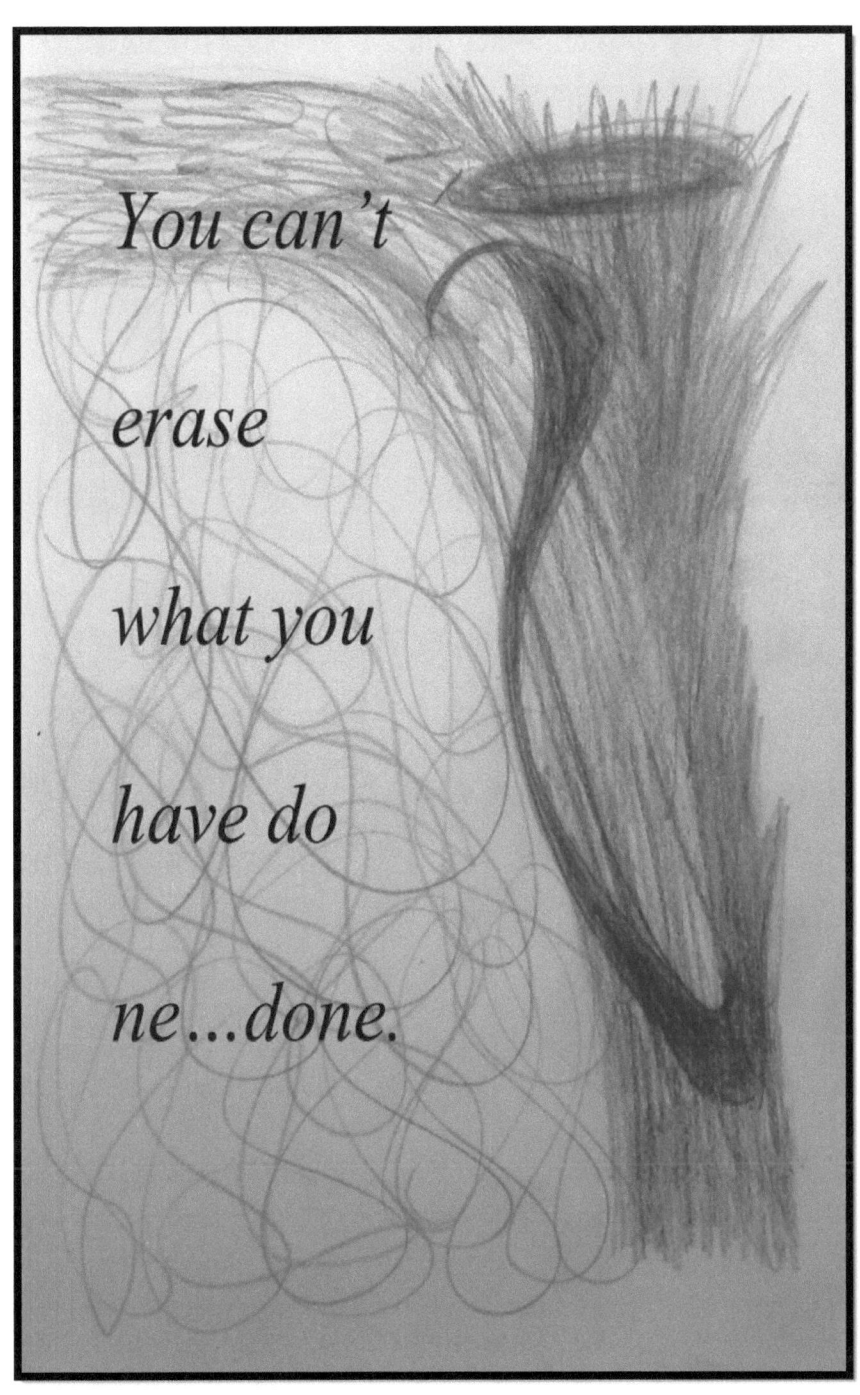

You can't

erase

what you

have do

ne...done.

It is a big mix of pictures. I think everyone will agree. A lot of different types. It makes sense. There are a lot of different messages they are sending through my arte…art. *Arty? Do you have a message, too?*

"I love the things that cannot be explained. They challenge us. They strain our minds, bend our hearts, and open our eyes. Even better yet, I love when the unexpected occurs. The unexpected in a mundane life. A life well on its course takes a turn in a direction that a month prior could have never been seen or even dreamed. "Do you believe in spirits?" I asked my friend. "Ghosts, you mean?" he replied. "No…spirits of people who have died." "Well look", he said, "I believe there are things that can't be explained." That was all I needed to hear…and I began to pour out ALL my stories…" Excerpt from "Chapel Street Signs". The beginning.

And pour I did. I will be almost up to 300,000 words by the end of "Hand of Heven".

About the Author and *Illustrator*

RL Lane has published the EcarreT series and a collection of art books featuring the illustrations throughout the books. The series begins with "Chapel Street Signs"…

…unexplained connections that challenge us to beli ve. A woman, a Dad a Doctor, a cat and mouse, a horse and tale tell their stories. "Do you beli ve in spirits?" I asked my friend. "Well look", he said, "I believe there are things that cannot be explained…" Oh. Plus, hear ov a Mom's battle with her struggle to connect to the woman…her little girl.

Welcome to EcarreT…a world
Where everyone cares
Why did I have to create it in…

A fiction fantasy world?

You may already know why, but you will see regardless of what you believe as a girl's journey of love and faith on her "Touring Machine" take her on the best journey of her mundane life. A life well on its way takes a turn in a direction that could've never been seen or even dreamed…

The author can be contacted at:

RosaLeeeLane@gmail.com
www.Amazon.com/author/readrllane

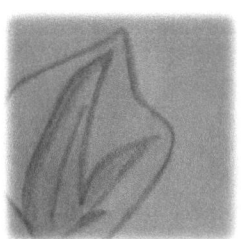

www.ingramcontent.com/pod-product-compliance
Lightning Source LLC
Chambersburg PA
CBHW050433180526

45159CB00006B/2514